HAL•LEONARD
INSTRUMENTAL PLAY-ALONG

TROMBONE

MOTOWN CLASSICS

T0081999

HOW TO USE THE CD ACCOMPANIMENT:

A MELODY CUE APPEARS ON THE RIGHT CHANNEL ONLY.
IF YOUR CD PLAYER HAS A BALANCE ADJUSTMENT, YOU CAN ADJUST THE VOLUME
OF THE MELODY BY TURNING DOWN THE RIGHT CHANNEL.

THE CD IS PLAYABLE ON ANY CD PLAYER, AND IS ALSO ENHANCED SO MAC AND PC USERS
CAN ADJUST THE RECORDING TO ANY TEMPO WITHOUT CHANGING THE PITCH!

ISBN: 978-1-4584-0562-3

HAL•LEONARD®
CORPORATION
7777 W. BLUEMOUND RD. P.O. BOX 13819 MILWAUKEE, WI 53213

Visit Hal Leonard Online at
www.halleonard.com

CONTENTS

◆ ABC

TROMBONE

Words and Music by ALPHONSO MIZELL,
FREDERICK PERREN, DEKE RICHARDS
and BERRY GORDY

5

❷ AIN'T NO MOUNTAIN HIGH ENOUGH

TROMBONE

Words and Music by NICKOLAS ASHFORD
and VALERIE SIMPSON

❸ BABY LOVE

TROMBONE

Words and Music by BRIAN HOLLAND,
EDWARD HOLLAND and LAMONT DOZIER

◆ ENDLESS LOVE

TROMBONE

Words and Music by
LIONEL RICHIE

◆ HOW SWEET IT IS

(To Be Loved by You)

TROMBONE

Words and Music by EDWARD HOLLAND,
LAMONT DOZIER and BRIAN HOLLAND

◆ I CAN'T HELP MYSELF
(Sugar Pie, Honey Bunch)

TROMBONE

Words and Music by BRIAN HOLLAND,
LAMONT DOZIER and EDWARD HOLLAND

7 I JUST CALLED TO SAY I LOVE YOU

TROMBONE

Words and Music by
STEVIE WONDER

◆8 I'LL BE THERE

TROMBONE

Words and Music by BERRY GORDY,
HAL DAVIS, WILLIE HUTCH
and BOB WEST

Moderately

Harpsichord

MY CHERIE AMOUR

TROMBONE

Words and Music by STEVIE WONDER,
SYLVIA MOY and HENRY COSBY

THREE TIMES A LADY

TROMBONE

Words and Music by
LIONEL RICHIE

⓫ MY GIRL

TROMBONE

Words and Music by WILLIAM "SMOKEY" ROBINSON
and RONALD WHITE

STOP! IN THE NAME OF LOVE

TROMBONE

Words and Music by LAMONT DOZIER,
BRIAN HOLLAND and EDWARD HOLLAND

⑬ THE TRACKS OF MY TEARS

TROMBONE

Words and Music by WILLIAM "SMOKEY" ROBINSON,
WARREN MOORE and MARVIN TARPLIN

◆14 WHAT'S GOING ON

TROMBONE

Words and Music by RENALDO BENSON,
ALFRED CLEVELAND and MARVIN GAYE

⑮ YOU'VE REALLY GOT A HOLD ON ME

TROMBONE

Words and Music by
WILLIAM "SMOKEY" ROBINSON